West by Covered Wagon

TO THE MILLER FAMILY AND FORREST DAVIS, WITH APPRECIATION.
— D. H. P. AND W. M.

First published in the United States of America in 1995 by Walker Publishing Company, Inc.

Published simultaneously in Canada by Thomas Allen & Son Canada,
Limited, Markham, Ontario

Library of Congress Cataloging-in-Publication Data
Patent, Dorothy Hinshaw.
West by covered wagon : retracing the pioneer trails / Dorothy
Hinshaw Patent ; photographs by William Muñoz.
p.   cm.
ISBN 0-8027-8377-5 (hardcover). — ISBN 0-8027-8378-3 (reinforced)
1. Overland journeys to the Pacific—Juvenile literature. 2. West
(U.S.)—Description and travel—Juvenile literature. 3. Trails—
West (U.S.)—History—19th century—Juvenile literature.
[1. Overland journeys to the Pacific. 2. West (U.S.)—
History 1848–1860.] I. Muñoz, William, ill. II. Title.
F593.P35   1995
978'.02—dc20   94-48233
CIP   AC

Book design by Diane Stevenson of Snap-Haus Graphics

Printed in Hong Kong

2   4   6   8   10   9   7   5   3   1

WEST BY COVERED WAGON

RETRACING THE PIONEER TRAILS

DOROTHY HINSHAW PATENT Photographs by **WILLIAM MUÑOZ**

WALKER AND COMPANY   NEW YORK

✥ Introduction ✥

During the 1800s, when the United States was still a young country, many people wanted to move west. Going west was a way for the restless, the unlucky, or the poor to start a new life. The western lands were not states yet. Some were territories—they belonged to the United States but were not yet accepted into the union as states. Others were not even territories. A pioneer who settled in Oregon before 1846 didn't know if his new home would end up as part of the United States or in a different country.

Settlers in Oregon or in the territories could claim land for themselves. By living on the land and working it as a farm or ranch for a few years, the settlers earned title to the land. It became theirs.

THE PIONEERS HAD TO CROSS HUNDREDS OF MILES OF PRAIRIE BEFORE REACHING THE ROCKY MOUNTAINS (FACING PAGE).

Getting to the West wasn't easy. There were no cars or trucks and no highways. So people had to travel the hard way. They put a supply of food, some possessions, and their children in a wagon. Then they joined other people heading west for a grueling journey through unfamiliar and sometimes dangerous lands.

Trails went west to different parts of the country. But the main route was the famous Oregon Trail, which led to Oregon's Willamette Valley, with a branch south to California. It began as a route for fur traders, adventurers, and missionaries. It required 2,000 miles of slow travel, which meant leaving Missouri, where the trail began, in April or May and arriving in Oregon four and a half or more months later. Wagon travel on the Oregon Trail began in the early 1840s. By 1848, more than 14,000 pioneers had made the journey. People continued to travel along the trail in large numbers through the 1850s and 1860s. In 1869, a railroad connecting the East Coast to the West Coast was completed, making travel west much faster and easier. But still, the Oregon Trail was used as late as 1880.

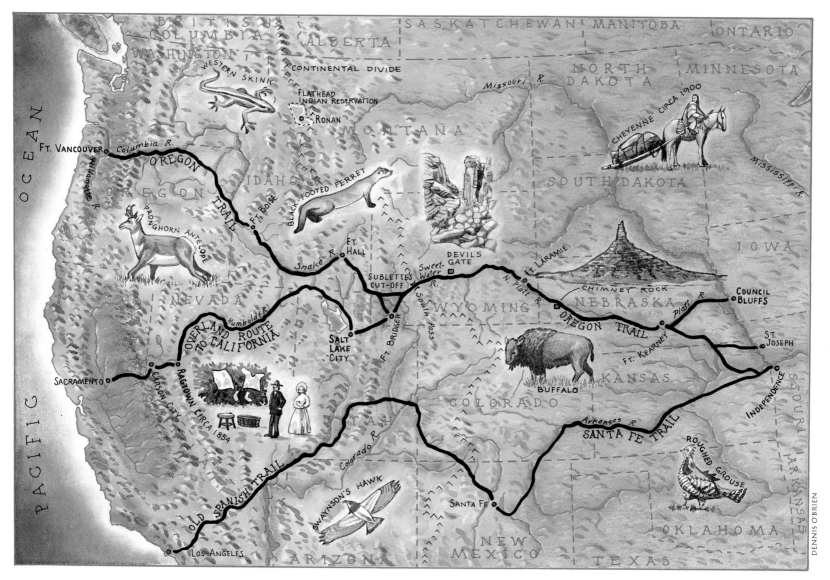

THE OLD OVERLAND TRAILS TO THE WEST. THE WESTMONT WAGONEERS' MODERN JOURNEY TAKES PLACE ON THE FLATHEAD
INDIAN RESERVATION IN WESTERN MONTANA, NEAR THE TOWN OF RONAN.

A COVERED WAGON BUILT BY PAT MILLER AND HIS FAMILY.

⇥ Reliving the Past ⇤

T he pioneers traveled because they wanted a better life and felt that going west was the only way to get it. They took their families and what few possessions they could fit into a wagon and headed west. What was it like to travel for months over wide, treeless prairies, across swift rivers, and over steep mountain passes? No one is now alive who made that dangerous, difficult journey. But some people today feel a strong connection with the pioneers. They enjoy the challenges involved in repairing old wagons and building new ones just like those used by pioneer families to cross the country. They train their horses and mules to work as teams to pull the wagons. In many parts of the country, these people get together for a few days to travel as their ancestors did, in wagons pulled by animals, across plains and mountains.

In western Montana, the Westmont Wagoneers have been taking a wagon ride on Memorial Day weekend for more than twenty years. About 200 people, who have as many as thirty-five wagons altogether, come from as far away as Iowa to participate. Many, like the Miller family, are farmers or ranchers who use horses to help in their work. But others are bankers, veterinarians, or other people with regular jobs who live on small farms and love horses.

THE WESTMONT WAGONEERS UNDER WAY THROUGH THE FLATHEAD INDIAN RESERVATION IN WESTERN MONTANA.

THE WAGONEERS' ENCAMPMENT BESIDE THE FLATHEAD RIVER.

CLARA MILLER HOLDS ONE OF HER TWIN
GRANDDAUGHTERS, WHO GOES ALONG
FOR THE RIDE.

For them, the Memorial Day trip provides a rare opportunity to work with their horses and experience a little outdoor life. Everyone who goes along gets a chance to catch up with family and friends, share stories, and make good memories. The peace and quiet of the countryside and the opportunity to sleep under the stars, away from the cares of ordinary life, renew the wagoneers' spirits.

The Miller family grew up with horses. Pat and Clara raised their nine children on a farm with all kinds of animals. Every year, their own Percheron horses pull their wagons through the countryside on Memorial Day weekend, with plenty of family members along to join in the fun.

HORSES LIKE THIS PERCHERON, OWNED BY THE MILLERS, ARE MOST COMMONLY USED TO PULL WAGONS TODAY.

⇥ Animal Power ⇤

Without strong animals, the pioneer wagons couldn't go anywhere. Oxen were the most reliable draft animals. They could survive well on the poor grass that might be the only pasture encountered along the trail. Horses needed better grazing and wore out quickly.

Mules were stronger than horses and moved faster than oxen. But they could be stubborn, and they sometimes stampeded, running away and leaving their owners helpless. Oxen were slow but steady. They were very strong and even-tempered. A typical pioneer family wagon required at least four mules or oxen to pull it. Six could do the job better.

On the Westmont Wagoneers' ride, the wagons are usually pulled by horses, like the Millers' Percherons, or mules. Because the wagons are not heavily loaded and because the ride is short, two to four animals make a big enough team. People now often ride horseback beside the wagons. Horses and mules can also carry extra supplies. But back when the original settlers went west, the cost of horses and the need to feed them while traveling meant that many folks walked most of the way across the continent. Pioneer wagon trains needed extra oxen and mules to replace animals that needed a rest or died. Other livestock, such as milk cows, might also be brought along. The older boys herded the extra stock along the trail. When the women and younger children got tired of riding in the jolting wagons, they gave the boys a break and took care of the stock.

TYPICAL COVERED WAGONS HAVE BIG
WHEELS TO MAKE PULLING EASIER FOR
THE ANIMALS. THE WAGON BODY, OR
"BOX," IS FOUR FEET WIDE AND TEN TO
TWELVE FEET LONG. IT RIDES HIGH OFF
THE GROUND TO KEEP IT FROM SCRAPING
ON ROUGH ROADS. TO KEEP ITEMS FROM
ROLLING OR SPILLING, THE ENDS OF THE
BOX ARE HIGHER THAN THE MIDDLE.

HORSES CAN CARRY EXTRA PEOPLE
AND EXTRA SUPPLIES.

13

SEAN MUÑOZ (SITTING ON PICNIC BENCH) JOINS THE MILLERS IN THEIR COMFORTABLE CAMP.

� Getting Organized ⟩⟩

Today, the people traveling on a wagon train gather their food and equipment at home. They can bring along canned goods and other convenience foods, plus refrigerated food in coolers. They have to take only enough to eat for a few days. Unlike the pioneers, they don't need to bring all their belongings. All they need are sleeping bags, folding chairs, and maybe a tent. They drive in cars and trucks to the rendezvous site where the ride begins, carrying their animals in horse trailers.

Pioneers planning to take the Oregon Trail arrived in Independence or St. Joseph, Missouri, without many goods

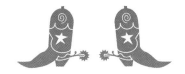

except for their most prized possessions and heirlooms. Some had wagons to be converted, but others bought everything they needed for the trip at the starting point. Both towns bustled with activity, with people selling wagons, food, clothing, firearms, and other vital items, and auctioneers selling mules, horses, and oxen.

It takes time to get a wagon ready to travel. It must be carefully loaded, for there isn't much room inside. The pioneers had to fit in not only food for many weeks but also important items like a stove, a butter churn, and a plow, which they'd need to start a new home.

By the end of the journey west, the pioneers were quite bored by the simple diet they had to eat along the trail.

PAT MILLER AND HIS SON, GALE, PUT THE FINISHING TOUCHES ON A WAGON. COVERED WAGONS ARE BUILT TO BE STRONG AND STURDY, NOT COMFORTABLE. THEY BOUNCE, RATTLE, AND SWAY WITH EVERY ROCK AND RUT, SO RIDING IN THE BOX IS VERY UNCOMFORTABLE. THE SEAT IN FRONT, HOWEVER, HAS METAL BOWS THAT SERVE AS SPRINGS TO EASE THE BOUNCING AND BUMPING.

A TYPICAL COVERED WAGON WAS
NARROW AND COULD STORE ONLY
LIMITED QUANTITIES OF GOODS. CAN
YOU IMAGINE PUTTING ALL YOUR
FAMILY'S POSSESSIONS IN SUCH
A SMALL SPACE?

Food supplies for the Oregon Trail trip for each adult consisted of 200 pounds of flour, a half-bushel of dried beans, ten pounds of rice, seventy-five pounds of bacon, twenty-five pounds of sugar, two pounds of baking soda, thirty pounds of flat crackerlike bread, two pounds of tea, a bushel of dried fruit, ten pounds of salt, a half-bushel of corn meal, and five pounds of coffee. Other foods, such as coarsely ground corn and vinegar, might also be brought along.

Underneath the wagon hung a bucket of grease for the wheels. Another bucket contained coals from the last night's fire, since the pioneers had no matches. They lacked other conveniences we take for granted, too, such as mosquito

HITCHING UP THE TEAM TAKES TIME AND EFFORT.

repellent and sunblock lotion to protect them from the discomforts of the trail. Rugged clothing, boots, blankets, goods to trade with the Indians for food or clothing, and a rifle for hunting game were also standard equipment.

As the wagons traveled, some of the men would venture in different directions on horseback to hunt. During the early years of settlement, game was relatively abundant, so the pioneers could hope for a meal including buffalo or antelope now and then. But as the years went by, game became more and more difficult to find.

Water was the most precious commodity of all through some stretches of the western trails, for people and animals alike. Travel was timed to reach water at noon and before sunset each day. Only small amounts of water could be carried along, because it added too much weight. Fouled or alkaline water caused deaths along the trail when good water was not to be found.

Wagoneers today must bring their drinking water along with them, because water from rivers and streams can contain dangerous parasites that make people sick. A wooden barrel lined with plastic to keep it from leaking carries the Millers' drinking water. In pioneer times, travelers had to rely on fine workmanship to make containers watertight so they would not lose precious liquid.

THE WATER BARREL, WITH ITS MODERN PLASTIC LINING, IS READY FOR MORNING WASH-UP.

WHEN TODAY'S WAGONS GO OUT, THEY
MUST SOMETIMES DEAL WITH CARS
STIRRING UP DUST ON THE ROAD.

⇥ On the Road ⇤

Today, wagon trains travel mostly down country roads. The roads are generally not paved, but they are usually smooth. Even so, a person riding in the wagon can feel every bump, rock, and pothole as the wagon rolls along. Now and then a car passes by, swirling up extra dust. The dust blew back then, too, stirred by wind and wheels and settling inside the wagons and inside the travelers' lungs.

Most pioneers traveled in groups. The earliest ones hired guides to show them the way. Sometimes it was difficult to figure out the best places to cross rivers and mountain ranges. But later, ruts across the prairie and piles of debris

showed the way clearly, and guidebooks became available. Even so, a wagon train always needed a captain. He was usually chosen by a democratic vote, and the travelers pledged to abide by his decisions, although disagreements broke out often and sometimes led to wagon trains splitting up. The captain determined the order of the wagons in the train. He assigned some men to be outriders, who kept an eye out for trouble. He decided when and where the group stopped for lunch and overnight.

THE WAGONS THEMSELVES CAN ALSO CREATE UNPLEASANT DUST CLOUDS.

Although wagon rides today are much simpler than pioneer wagon trains, an organizer, now called the wagon master, is still a necessity. Pat Miller has often taken on those duties—clearing permission from property owners along the route, checking to see that all the wagons are properly and safely equipped, and hauling in water and hay when necessary. When problems arise, the wagon master tries to help solve them. Another person called the trail boss helps deal with difficulties that occur during the ride.

RIDERS ON HORSEBACK CAN GALLOP AHEAD TO SCOUT OUT THE LAND.

The routes used by the pioneers started as faint marks
across the prairie grasses. They built up, one set of tracks at
a time. As more and more wagons used the same trails, they
became like dirt roads. Thousands and thousands of wagons,
year after year of tramping hooves, storm after storm
dropping rain that turned dirt into mud and washed it away—
all led to the wearing away of the trails. The ruts grew deeper
and deeper, especially on slopes, until the wagons could
barely clear the center of the road. Where possible, travelers
fanned out to avoid the ruts and dust. Along flatter stretches,
the Oregon Trail became up to twenty miles wide, its
direction marked by faint wagon tracks across the prairie.

HORSES' HOOVES SOMETIMES NEED TENDING.

Crossing the mountains was very hard for the heavily loaded wagons. On the steepest passes, the wagons were pulled slowly uphill, using ropes and pulleys. With each bit of forward progress, rocks were placed behind the back wheels to keep the wagon from going backward. After the pass was reached, the wagons had to be carefully held back as they went down the other side.

ALTHOUGH THE HILLS THEY MUST CLIMB ARE NOT AS CHALLENGING AS THOSE ENCOUNTERED BY THE PIONEERS, THE MILLERS TAKE PRIDE IN BEING ABLE TO GET UP AND OVER THE STEEPEST PARTS OF THE TRAIL WITHOUT HELP FROM OTHER TEAMS.

⇒ Setting the Pace ⇐

In frontier times, the wagons went fifteen to twenty miles in a day. Traveling at a good, steady pace was very important, for the plains had to be crossed while the grass on the prairie was still green to provide enough food for the hardworking animals. If a wagon train began the long trek too early, the grass was too sparse for feed and the ground could be too soggy. And if the train traveled too late, summertime drought could have killed the grass, for on the plains, summer temperatures could soar above 100° F.

Late travelers also risked meeting blizzards in the mountain passes that could make the trails impassable and make even survival difficult, as the thermometer could drop below zero.

As long as the travelers made good time, however, the captain might decide that they could take an extra day or two in camp now and then to do laundry, hunt, and rest the animals. Stops were not always a matter of choice. If a wagon broke down, the whole train had to stop and wait until repairs were made.

The pioneers had to expect all sorts of weather, which could also interrupt the timing of travel. The plains could send up choking dust storms, so severe that the animals couldn't breathe well enough to pull the wagons. Sudden violent thunderstorms could make rivers rise too high to cross; the settlers would have to camp nearby and wait until the water level dropped, which sometimes took as long as two weeks.

Crossing rivers was often a major hazard. Sometimes the rivers flowed too high for wagons to cross on their wheels. In that case, the wheels were removed, the wagon boxes were waterproofed with buffalo skins or pitch, and the wagons floated across like awkward, flat-bottomed boats. But all of this was risky. A simple miscalculation could result in disaster.

THE CANVAS TOP IS HELD UP BY HOOPS MADE OF FLEXIBLE WOOD, SUCH AS HICKORY. IT PROTECTS THE GOODS AND PEOPLE INSIDE THE WAGON FROM THE WEATHER. THE ENDS OF THE TOP CAN BE CLOSED OFF OR OPENED UP. A CLOSED TOP HOLDS IN THE WARMTH ON A COLD DAY AND HELPS KEEP OUT DUST, WHILE AN OPEN ONE LETS IN A COOL BREEZE WHEN IT IS SUNNY AND HOT.

FRESH GRASS TO FEED HARDWORKING ANIMALS WAS CRITICAL TO THE SUCCESS OF THE PIONEER WAGON TRAINS (FACING PAGE; INSET).

THE TOP CAN BE MOVED OFF THE FRONT HOOP DURING GOOD WEATHER, AS FORREST DAVIS HAS DONE HERE (FACING PAGE).

Many a pioneer family watched in horror as their wagon sank, carrying with it all their possessions and food for the journey. Many lives were lost as well. In 1850, one treacherous crossing of the Platte River near Fort Laramie, in what is now the state of Wyoming, took nineteen lives. A crossing farther down the trail brought about twenty-eight deaths in 1849 and twenty-one in 1850.

When storm clouds gathered, the captain had to decide whether to press onward to meet the goal for the day or stop and make camp before the torrents fell. To the pioneers, losing even a half-day could spell disaster if their timing was tight. But trying to forge ahead when the trail was thick with mud was risky because the wagons might bog down and get stuck, causing further delays.

WHEN STORM CLOUDS GATHERED, A DECISION HAD TO BE MADE ABOUT WHETHER TO CONTINUE OR MAKE CAMP.

THIS FOAL, WHICH DEPENDS ON ITS MOTHER FOR MILK, TAGS ALONG ON THE WAGON RIDE.

⇒ Life and Death on the Trail ⇐

Normal life continued on the trail. Babies were born, both to animals and people, and became instant travelers. Both people and animals died of disease or overwork. Rough graves dotted the routes of travel. The sight of so many graves seriously frightened the pioneers.

At least 20,000 pioneers did die along the Oregon Trail—one out of every seventeen people to attempt the journey. Disease caused nine out of ten deaths. The biggest killer was cholera. In both 1850 and 1852, at least 2,000 people on the trail died of this terrible disease.

When animals died, their bodies were simply left to rot, sometimes in large numbers. One pioneer wrote about a section of the trail near Scotts Bluff, Nebraska: "A traveler could find his way with no other compass or guide than his nose alone" because of all the rotting ox carcasses.

Today's wagoneers need not worry about such serious matters. Instead, these people may use a wagon trip to celebrate an important event. For the participants, the trip is the one time of the year when they are together with so many old friends and acquaintances who share the same memories of past journeys. The Millers use the annual event for a family reunion. The Westmont Wagoneers have also celebrated a wedding and many anniversaries, including one couple's sixty-seventh. One year, they scattered the ashes of a member who had passed away.

THE MILLERS' HORSES FEED ON HAY DURING THE TRIP.

PLASTIC TARPS MAKE SETTING UP EASY TODAY.

⇥ Making Camp ⇤

Making camp today is easier now than it was then. After a day on the trail, the Millers unhitch the horses and take them to water. Then they feed the horses hay, which is brought in ahead of time to each campsite. They set up their modern, lightweight tents and unfold their comfortable aluminum chairs. After putting fresh food from the cooler on the fire, they can pop open cans of cold soft drinks and snack on potato chips while their meal is cooking.

At the end of a day's travel, pioneer families were tired from walking or riding for miles. But they had work to do.

THE MILLER FAMILY PREFERS TRADITIONAL CANVAS TO PLASTIC. CANVAS STAYS IN PLACE BETTER WHEN THE WIND KICKS UP.

The men and boys circled the wagons, unhitched the animals, took them to water, then set them free to graze. The women and girls had to prepare the simple evening meal from scratch, while the younger children looked for buffalo chips—dried buffalo dung—as fuel for the fire. Sometimes the children turned the search into a competition, dashing about in an effort to be the one to collect the most fuel.

Some people brought along a canvas tent for sleeping, which took time to set up. Many pioneers simply slept under their wagon or under the stars, protected from dew by canvas folded over their blankets. There wasn't room inside the wagon for the whole family.

MULES WAIT PATIENTLY BESIDE A WAGON.

⇒ Journey's End ⇐

ONCE THE PIONEERS REACHED THEIR DESTINATIONS, THEY HAD TO GET RIGHT TO WORK MAKING THE LAND PRODUCTIVE FOR THEM. TODAY, SOME FARMERS, LIKE GORDI PASKE, STILL USE ANIMAL POWER INSTEAD OF MACHINES TO TILL THEIR FIELDS.

When the pioneers finally reached their destination, they were happy to give up the trail. Mary Burrell, who trekked to California in 1854, expressed what most pioneers must have felt. Arriving in Green Valley meant "ending a journey which for care, fatigue, tediousness, perplexities and dangers of various kinds can not be excelled."

But the pioneers' work had just begun. They had to build a house to shelter them for the winter, and they had to begin tilling the soil so they could plant crops.

The wagoneers of today often find that after just a few days on the trail, they wish they could stay out longer. The peace and quiet of the countryside and the companionship of friends and family are hard to give up. But they have settled lives and comfortable homes to return to. And they know that next year, they can hit the road again, renewing friendships, enjoying the beautiful western landscape, and sharing new adventures.

They swum the deep rivers and clumb the high peaks,
They rolled thro' the country for many long weeks,
Thro' all sorts of misery, dry days and wet,
If they hadn't gone on, they'd be campin' there yet.

"Sweet Betsy from Pike"
(American folk song)